ROBERT CAMERON'S
ALCATRAZ
A VISUAL ESSAY

A Collection of Historical and Contemporary
Photographs, Drawings and Paintings together with
Original Color Photography

Published by

Cameron and Company, Inc.
235 Montgomery Street, Suite 440
San Francisco, California 94104
415/981-1135   415/468-5255

Library of Congress Catalog Number: 74-18606

Alcatraz ISBN 0-918684-19-16

First Printing 1974

Revised Second Printing 1983

Color Photography
by
Robert Cameron

Text and Captions
by
Robert E. Burger

Book Design and Editing
by
Jane Olaug Kristiansen

Cameron and Company, Inc., San Francisco, California

This book could not have reached its final form without the valued cooperation of the following:

Hatsuro Aizawa
Pat Akre, San Francisco Public Library
The Bancroft Library
J. Campbell Bruce
Lee Burtis
Todd E. Cameron
Ann Campbell, The National Archives
Clarence (Joe) Carnes
Ken Cellini
Ken Chase
Phil Dollison
Albert Ellidge
Barbara Johnston Ford
William Ganslen
Dr. Floyd Gonella
Robert Guilford
Steve Hammond
Gladys Hansen, San Francisco Public Library
J.S. Holliday, California Historical Society
William Knott
Suzanne Thomas Lawlor
Dr. Mary Thomas Martinet
Patricia O'Grady
Jerry Rumburg, National Park Service
John Slavicek
Carol Thares

The publisher acknowledges with thanks the generous help of the following in furnishing many of the pictures in this book:

Ed DeMartini
International News Service
Germano Milono A.I.A.
Gabriel Moulin
Stanley A. Piltz
Peter S. Sabin A.I.A.
San Francisco Call Bulletin
        Howard Robbins
San Francisco Chronicle
        Clem Albers
        Vincent Maggiora
San Francisco Examiner
San Francisco News
H.H. Tammen Co.
United Artists
United Press International
Warner Brothers
Western Aerial Surveys

And he also acknowledges the artistry of those whose pictures appear anonymously because their origins cannot now be traced.

Typography by ReederType, Inc., Fremont, California
Color Separation and Printing by Dai Nippon Printing Co., Tokyo, Japan

TABLE OF CONTENTS

PAST   13

PRISON   35

PRISONERS   57

HOLLYWOOD   73

OCCUPATION   79

PRESENT   87

Adrift in the azure Bay, the Rock waits jealously offshore for its final definition in the San Francisco panorama. Now only the birds and an occasional aerial photographer see her in her tropical richness jutting cleanly from the waters. The prison has here been abandoned for six years, and the Indian occupation has yet to leave its mark.

ISLAND OF NO RETURN

The tarnished jewel which nature placed in San Francisco Bay has been coveted and feared, admired and discarded by successive generations since the day some two hundred years ago when the Spanish explorer Ayala gave it the name *Isla de Alcatraces*, island of pelicans. The thought keeps coming back that someone should "do something with it." This book is a pictorial essay on how man has wrestled with that thought and with those twelve acres of sandstone.

Call it Bird Island or The Rock or Alcatraz, it has patiently resisted every attempt to be made into something of lasting utility. As this chronicle will show in general order of time, it has been a lighthouse, a fort, every category of prison, a battleground, a tourist attraction—growing from one role into the next more by default than by design. We have tried to give it to the military, to force it on the outcasts of society, to return it to the people. Perhaps some day it will be taken back by nature.

The lighthouse, the last functioning structure on the island today, stands silently between the deserted administration building and the burnt out shell of the warden's house. The parade grounds below are gradually yielding to vegetation. Touring boats dock on the other side of the island (overleaf).

The Rock today with its barbed wire, crumbling concrete, steel towers and wood frame buildings is strangely out of step with the life around it. In the shadow of a flowering metropolis, it is a collection of over one hundred and forty years of architectural leftovers.

11

ALCATRAZ ISLAND 1856

PAST

There is little in the past of Alcatraz to sustain the legends of underground dungeons and mysterious confinements, yet the island has created a lively history of its own. Like the image on a photographic plate, it marked the Civil War by becoming a prison for Southern privateers, then, military recalcitrants, a confinement for troublesome Indians in the seventies, a depository of prisoners from the Spanish-American war at the turn of the century, a health resort for ailing rough-riders, a temporary city jail after the San Francisco earthquake in 1906, and, again, a military prison for espionage agents, enemy aliens and conscientious objecters during the first World War. Its birthday under its present name was August 5, 1775, but, apparently, it was not explored until 1846, when Julian Workman petitioned Pio Pico, Mexican governor of California to establish a navigational light on "a small island called Alcatraces, or Bird Island, which has never been inhabited by any person, nor used for any purpose." Before the claim could be effected, California had become part of the United States, the island was ceded to the government and a military role was mapped out for it. It was now part of history.

In 1856, a photograph across Meiggs Wharf, at the foot of Powell Street, shows Alcatraz to jibe with the first report of the Army Engineers in 1853, "a mass of rock with a very thin crust of soil and of bird manure on the surface." It was literally the "Isle of Pelicans."

This Indenture, made the Seventh day of

November one thousand eight hundred and fifty Six Between Joseph C Palmer of the City of San Francisco State of California, party of the first part and John C Fremont Esquire of Mariposas in said State of California of the second part, Witnesseth, That the said party of the first part, for and in consideration of the sum of One dollar and other good and valuable considerations lawful money of the United States of America, to him in hand paid by the said party of the second part, at or before the ensealing and delivery of these presents, the receipt whereof is hereby acknowledged, hath granted, bargained, sold, aliened, remised, released, conveyed and confirmed, and by these presents doth grant, bargain sell, alien, remise, release, convey and confirm, unto the said party of the second part, and to his ——— heirs and assigns for ever, **ALL** that certain Island known by the name of the Alcatrasses Island and commonly called White or Bird Island situate near the mouth of the Bay of San Francisco in the State of California ———

Together with all and singular the tenements, hereditaments and appurtenances thereunto belonging or in anywise appertaining, and the reversion and reversions, remainder and remainders, rents, issues and profits thereof: And also, all the estate, right, title, interest, property, possession, claim and demand whatsoever, as well in law as in equity, of the said party of the first part, of, in or to the above described premises, and every part and parcel thereof, with the appurtenances. To Have and to Hold all and singular the above mentioned and described premises, together with the appurtenances, unto the said party of the second part, his heirs and assigns, for ever In witness whereof the said party of the first part hath hereunto set his hand and seal the day and year first before written

Sealed and delivered in presence of

Joseph C Palmer

W. H. Grady

In 1856 the City got around to turning over "Alcatrasses" to John C. Fremont, apparently as the ranking military officer in the state, even though he had just lost the Presidential election to Buchanan and had not lived in California for at least a year. This curious document is further clouded by the fact that fortifications on the island had been under construction since 1853. Shag rocks westward from the island were dynamited in 1901 as a safety measure for San Francisco's booming shipping industry.

Looking down Jones and Taylor from Russian Hill is a sampling of early San Francisco hillside architecture, from cottages to manors, and the artist's catalog of sailing vessels. Alcatraz looms larger than life. Against the impermanence of wood frame structures in the city, it stood out like a temple.

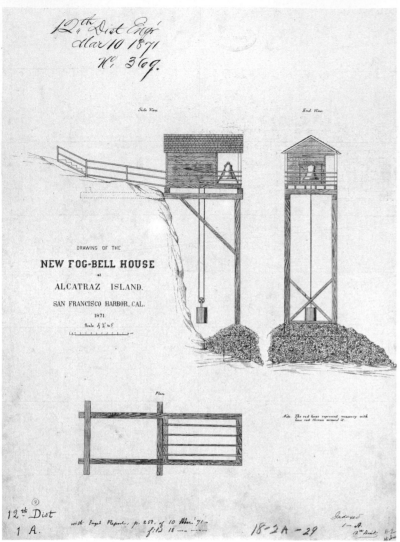

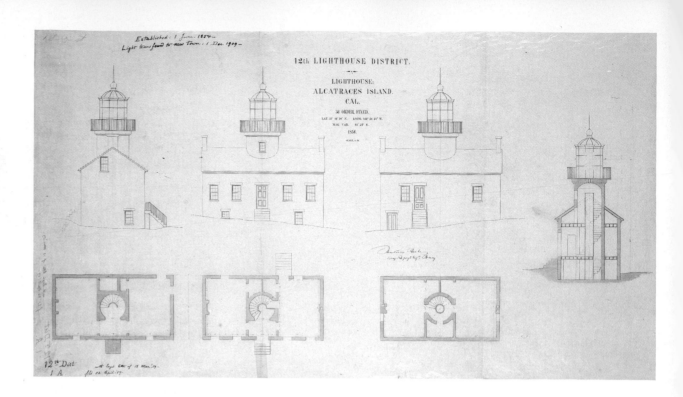

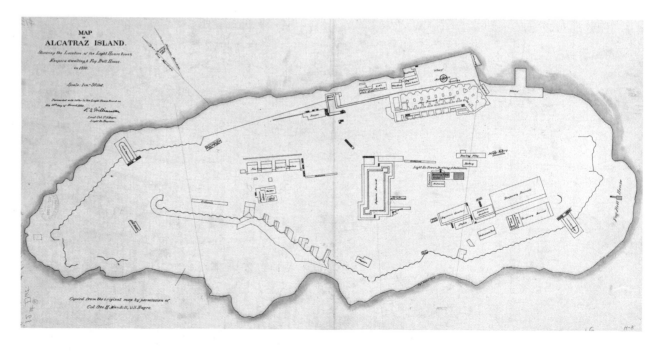

The beautifully proportioned lighthouse sent out its first beams through the Gate in 1854. A fog bell was added on the southeast end of the island in 1871. By 1880, a map of Alcatraz showed a dozen separate constructions. They were the main battery and observation "citadel" at the center, ramparts and officers' quarters to the left, lighthouse, bakery and bowling alley (even then!) to the right, below, the rambling group of barracks, engineers' quarters and stables (on the present parade grounds) and, at top near the wharf, a new, larger barracks under construction.

ALCATRAZ ISLAND

DEC. 1892

CHASEHRER

Another highly romantic view, with Angel Island looming in the background, dramatizes the brick fortress and quaint lighthouse. Has the western shore of the island eroded as much in ninety years as this 1892 painting would indicate? Note the fog bell, identifying the southeastern end of this seemingly idyllic isle.

Boat races off Meiggs Wharf were a popular entertainment in the 1860's. It was in these choppy waters that financier William Ralston drowned inexpllcably after his financial collapse in 1875. A magnificent oil painting of the "other" side of the island in 1880 seems to broaden the lighthouse level at the expense of truncating the "parade grounds."

Perhaps this threemaster had delivered a cargo of Civil War prisoners to the Rock. At the left is a drydock of the period, at North Point. This 1862 photograph says more about the tranquil northern shore of the City than about the island.

Black Point and Alcatraz, S. F., Cal.   1880

In 1886, "Black Point" or what is now generally North Beach also seemed an island. San Francisco and the Bay had yet to be filled in to its present contours. Angel Island in the background orients the photos. The painting of 1888 indicates how well built up, in contrast, was Alcatraz.

324. Ordnance Yard at Alcatraz Is.

164

319 French Admiral Cloué at Alcatraz

San Francisco From Alcatraz

The premier California photographer of the 19th century, Eadweard Muybridge, thought the fortifications of the Rock worth recording for posterity. These post-Civil War shots, now in the Bancroft Library on the other side of the Bay at the University of California, spread the early legend of an island fortress in the West.

616 *Arsenal & Ordnance Yard Alcatraz Island*

400 *Gardens on Alcatraz Island*

*Pacific Branch,
United States Military Prison
Alcatraz. Cal.*

For little boys and aging Napoleons, the cannonballs and rose gardens of Alcatraz were like phantasies of another era of war. These civilities soon vanished when it became a military prison. Ironically, among its guests were chiefs from the Indian wars that ended the century.

334 ALCATRAZ ISLAND

At the turn of the century, the island had taken on a well-designed look. Victorian buildings were nestled on the rock like filigreed cornices on a stately mansion as the hills and the port of the city were filling in.

Meanwhile, the island-city went its own way, not self-sufficient but self-contained, transformed from an arsenal into a military prison.

Fort Alcatraz.
San Francisco Bay.

You told me you had 71. Is this your 72nd?
Judith S.

S. F. 402. Alcatraz Island, San Francisco Bay, Cal.

S. F. 53. Alcatraz Island San Francisco. California. Copr. H. H. Tammen Co

U. S. Alcatraz Island, a Military Prison in San Francisco Bay.
Mt. Tamalpais in the Distance.

From its earliest days, Alcatraz was a "natural" for tourist postcards, some with crude attempts at humor.
On this and the two following pages, the photographers have explored the "East Bay" side of the
island, where the landing dock is the focus of a cluster of buildings at the water's edge, in every era.

San Francisco Bay - Alcatraz Island.

Alcatraz and Angel Islands from Nob Hill, San Francisco, Cal.

3055 ALCATRAZ ISLAND, SAN FRANCISCO BAY, CAL.

31:—ALCATRAZ ISLAND AND COIT TOWER, TELEGRAPH HILL, SAN FRANCISCO, CALIFORNIA

ALCATRAZ ISLAND, FEDERAL PRISON, SAN FRANCISCO BAY, CALIF.

11

© STANLEY A. PILTZ

6A-H86

"THE ROCK," ALCATRAZ ISLAND, SAN FRANCISCO, CALIF.—7

FOR SALE OR LEASE

Wish you were here!

These 1903 photographs by the government agency now in charge, the General Services Administration, chronicle the growth of lavatories, work rooms, chapel, mess hall, kitchen, hospital, and finally the prison. "It will be seen that the prisoners have no yard, no stockade, or other enclosure, but are, practically, free during the day…" a contemporary report read.

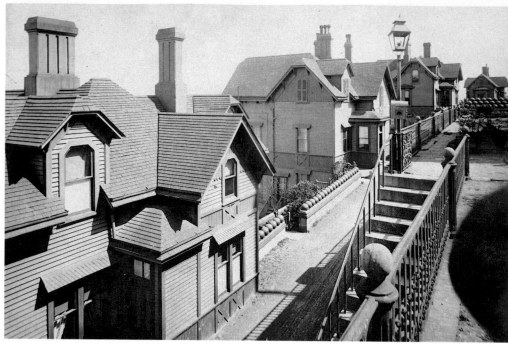

And to nourish the prison, a battery of support buildings were thrown up. A prominent building was the hospital. For the rest of the century, bit by bit, such evidence of self-sufficiency was to disappear until, at the height of prison activity, medical care was provided by a doctor's daily visit from San Francisco.

The pre-earthquake structures of brick and wood-frame were models of Victorian architecture, blending in agreeably with garrison buildings. The original 1854 lighthouse had become the post office by 1904.

The first mess hall could seat 200, yet, as early as 1903, two or three seatings were required to feed the prisoners—military incorrigibles and the detritus of the Spanish- American war and the Indian wars.

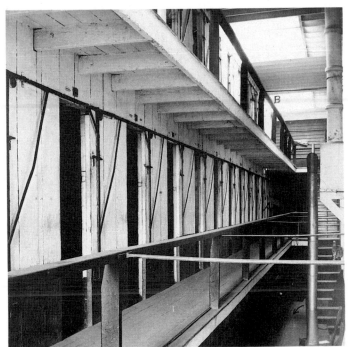

Pressure for reconstruction of detention areas began growing, as a federal report branded these facilities "dark, small, decaying" in 1903. When an oil lamp overturned, the shack-like cells almost went up.

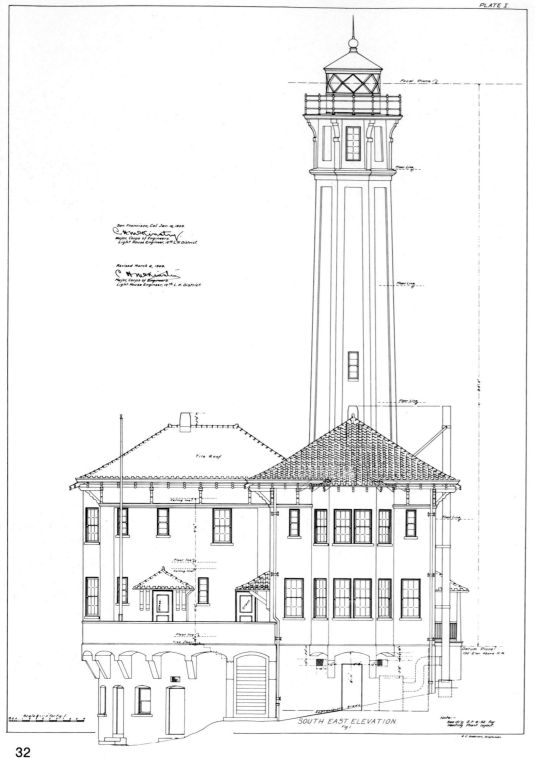

SOUTH EAST ELEVATION.
Fig. 1

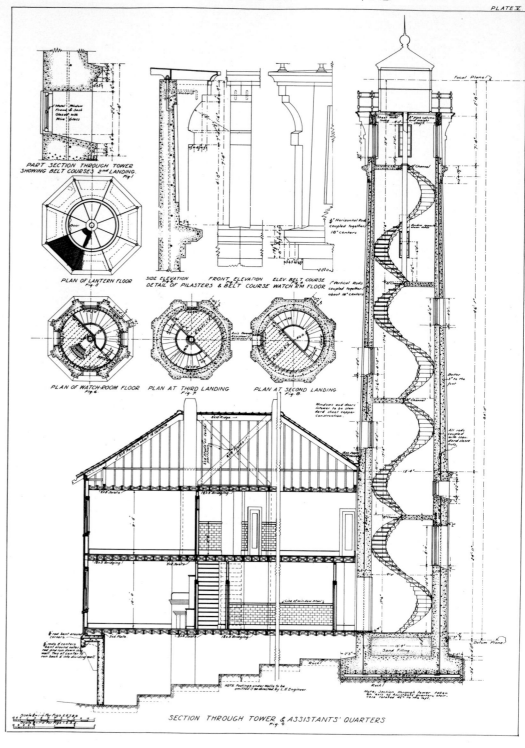

PART SECTION THROUGH TOWER
SHOWING BELT COURSES 2ND LANDING.
Fig. 1

PLAN OF LANTERN FLOOR
Fig. 5

SIDE ELEVATION   FRONT ELEVATION   ELEV. BELT COURSE
DETAIL OF PILASTERS & BELT COURSE WATCH R'M FLOOR

PLAN OF WATCH-ROOM FLOOR
Fig. 6

PLAN AT THIRD LANDING
Fig. 7

PLAN AT SECOND LANDING
Fig. 8

SECTION THROUGH TOWER & ASSISTANTS' QUARTERS
Fig. 4

The San Francisco earthquake of 1906 opened a fissure in The Rock but left the buildings unscathed. The City sent its overflow of prisoners to the island for temporary safekeeping. Triumphant, Fort Alcatraz now became Alcatraz Island, and the long awaited construction of new prison buildings was completed between 1906 and 1909. Interiors looked like this in 1911. The present main prison building and most of its support structures date from this period. Other than necessary manual labor, prisoners' work consisted of light crafts such as sewing and woodworking.

As World War I loomed, the facilities were ominously renamed U.S. Disciplinary Barracks. But the function of the island under the War Department was tenuous. The island would drift into uselessness for twenty years, until another federal agency would see in its cold, grey aloofness a new reason for existence.

In 1909, the present stately tower was built. Only the foundation under the grand, two-story lightkeeper's house now remains from the fires of 1969.

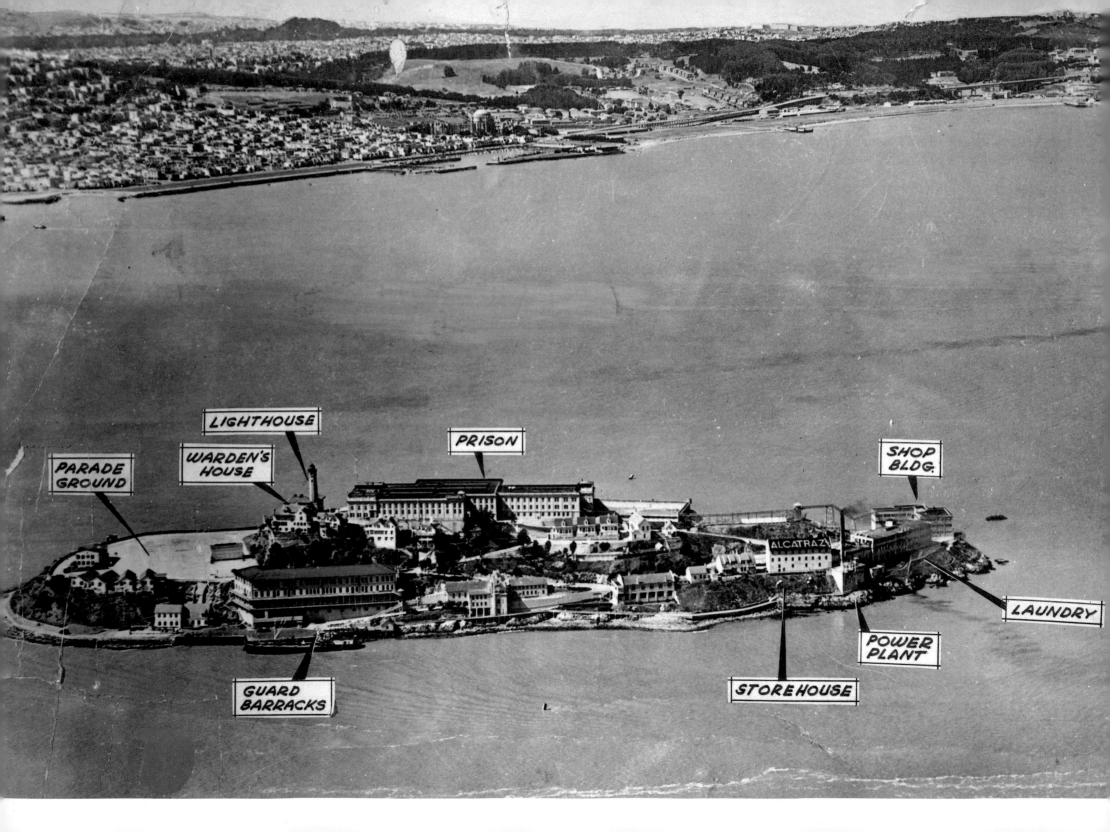

PARADE GROUND

LIGHTHOUSE

WARDEN'S HOUSE

PRISON

SHOP BLDG.

ALCATRAZ

LAUNDRY

POWER PLANT

STOREHOUSE

GUARD BARRACKS

PRISON

In 1934, on the second day of the year, Warden James A. Johnston took command of the island and began preparations for an experiment in penology. There was no sinister design in the idea of a maximum security prison in the middle of the most beautiful bay in the country, with the bright lights of freedom flickering offshore. It was an accident of the passage of time. The War Department announced that its fortifications had served their purpose without a shot having been fired since 1850, and the Justice Department could find no better place to house the recalcitrants from the gangster era. Tool-proof steel replaced the soft metal cell fronts that had been enough since 1909. Observation towers, gun galleries, barbed wire fences and electrically controlled gates were installed. Here and there, a Victorian structure would be allowed to remain, last of all, the warden's house. New buildings of 1930's gracelessness sprang up on the parade grounds to support a legion of guards. The original prison buildings on the acropolis had the dignity of ancient ruins and were now ready to receive hand-picked incorrigibles from the nation's penitentiaries.

Smoke from the power plant signalled the start of a new era for the island.

As the prison took shape, the Bay too was undergoing a transformation. The Golden Gate Bridge and the San Francisco-Oakland Bay Bridge were opened, dooming the train ferries. Now the prisoners would be able to watch a stream of lights on all four sides, as well as pleasure boats of all kinds. Soon came the World's Fair to nearby Treasure Island.

Warden Johnston, after whom the last launch to serve the prison was named, was meticulous in his security precautions. In seven months he had transformed a quiet army barracks into a fortress that would send chills through the prison-breakers, those that McNeil and Leavenworth and Atlanta could not hold. After a grand opening ceremony and inspection, word was flashed to Atlanta to start the first trainload of prisoners. It was August 19, 1934.

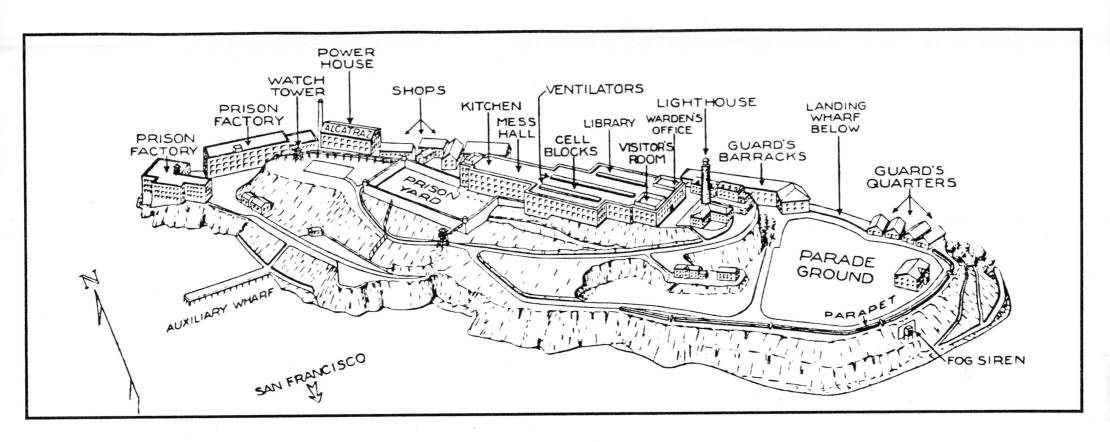

PRISON FACTORY · PRISON FACTORY · WATCH TOWER · POWER HOUSE · SHOPS · KITCHEN · MESS HALL · VENTILATORS · CELL BLOCKS · LIBRARY · VISITOR'S ROOM · WARDEN'S OFFICE · LIGHTHOUSE · GUARD'S BARRACKS · LANDING WHARF BELOW · GUARD'S QUARTERS

ALCATRAZ

PRISON YARD

PARADE GROUND

PARAPET

FOG SIREN

N

AUXILIARY WHARF

SAN FRANCISCO

The prison island from the San Francisco side in the mid-thirties.

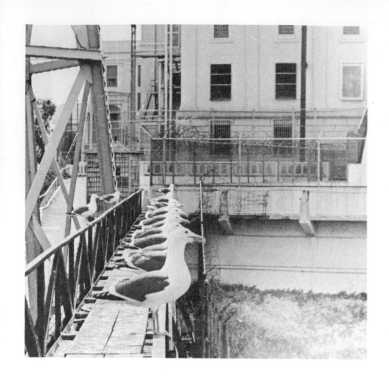

The prisoners came manacled in special trainloads across the country several days ahead of schedule as a precautionary measure. The cars were ferried intact from Tiburon to the island for "store front" delivery of their cargo, as the Bay's gulls looked on. It was once again "bird island." Jaunty, money-proud Al Capone felt the first ferry ride seal him off from his underworld to a life of discipline he would leave, dazed and ailing, in less than five years.

One of the first attempts at testing the defenses of Alcatraz came in 1938 when Rufus Jackson and Jimmy Lucas (arrows) overpowered and killed a guard, but failed to penetrate the outside walls. An accomplice was shot down and they were sentenced to life imprisonment. The "stool pigeon" that greeted new arrivals from shore electrically detected any weapons, but the worst symbol of confinement was the guard tower.

41

MARCH 13 1956
2 GRILLED FRANKFURTERS
1 HOT CHILI
PARSLEY POTATOES
POT FRIED SAUERKRAUT
BUTTERED CARROTS
1 MUSTARD
1 BANANA PUDDING
2 FRANKFURTER ROLLS

BREAD & TEA

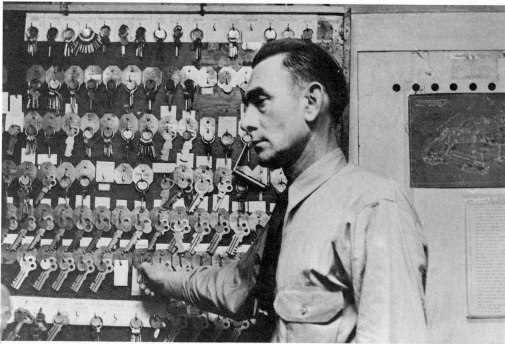

Food is one of the few remaining pleasures in confinement, and the prison administration took pains to reduce tension by providing some vestige of cuisine. Stories of mistreatment are belied by the menus. At first, prisoners were docked a meal for not cleaning their plates; later, this and the luxury of conversation were freely allowed.

One of the early confrontations, which reached proportions of a strike, was a protest against the required prison garb of overalls. Prisoners somehow felt better in trousers as they went about their tasks or strolled in the exercise yard. Recreation included an orchestra complete with another kind of uniform.

Alcatraz would become an anachronism in its own time, a showcase of buildings without faces, viewed through telescopes from Fisherman's Wharf for a nickel. It was no longer a part of the Bay. It was an attraction, a museum piece only a decade old.

Before there were regular visitors to the Rock, its maze of buildings could not be deciphered. Residents of the Bay Area gazed over it daily without ever knowing where the cells were, where the launch docked, where the prisoners played baseball. The cannons were easier to identify. In their later days, all of the structures on Alcatraz were, to the eye of the camera, simply PRISON.

 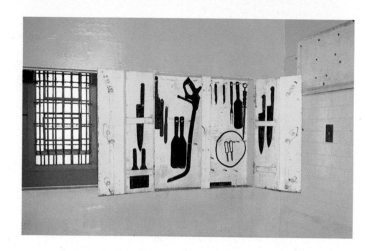 

But now we can see where life went on, even in this artificial, Robinson Crusoe isolation. Here are the occasional tropical flowers, the homes where guards and their families lived out a treacherous existence, and the cages of the men who made them all prisoners of this island.

The survivors of Alcatraz have agreed that it was the greyness of the island that chilled, as much as the incessant foghorns and the enveloping cold, wet winds. Warden Johnston had the cell blocks painted bright colors, but the gloom remained. Even the later guards' apartments facing San Francisco were said to have been as grey as the nearby prison factory.

The discipline of the cellblock was what Johnston expected to "whittle them down to size." The prisoners were to know they were behind bars—alone, muzzled, subject to severe penalties for stepping out of line. The charges of cruelty, covered up in secrecy, have never been documented beyond the allegations of prisoners in the dock and of newspaper reporters searching for a story. Cruelty did not have to be invented; there was enough in the grimness of confinement. There were some basement cells left over from the early army prison (not from the Spanish era); they were reserved for solitary confinement for such offenses as beating up a guard. Dungeons they were, with crude, wet concrete floors over the old cisterns and crumbling brick walls with chains newly installed, because prisoners could dig through them in a matter of days. This was the Dark Hole, where men like Clarence Carnes spent 19 days at a time in blackness. But, for those who toed the line there were clean cells, an infirmary, a library and a variety of occupations other than the "sweatshop" of the military era.

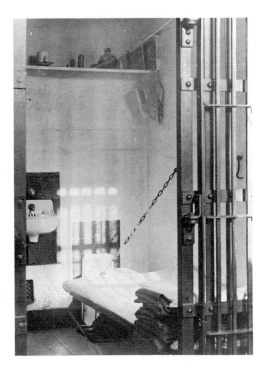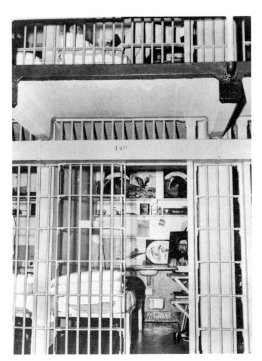

San Francisco News
San Francisco Cal

Please investigate criminal cruelty practices on prisoners at Alcatraz Prison. A few of the cases are (1) Edgar Lewis, age 28, serving 3 ys sentence, kept in dungeon for a total of more than 6 wks, starved, shot in face with gas gun, beaten over head with clubs by three guards (names will be given to investigating committe). He is now insane and is kept in a cage in the hospital. No hope for his recovery. His family lives at Los Banos, Calif. They don't know about it yet. The warden naturally wont give out information that will hang himself, but if an investigation is made and the inmates are questioned you will get the evidence. Another case is Jos. Bowers also insane from same cause, but not as bad condition as Lewis. James Grave is also insane and is under mental observation. John Stadeg is

Letters "exposing" cruelty on Alcatraz, like the one shown here smuggled to the San Francisco News in 1935, were usually retracted and charges were never documented. In a recent photo at night, the prison appears to be a quiet residential street in the city. But visiting some of the older rooms of the structure, especially where the old prison was dug out of rock, is disquieting.

Though long lines of prisoners were often visible going to and from tasks, the record shows that the prison capacity of 600 was more than twice actual occupancy in the twenty-six years of its operation from 1935 to 1960, shortly before it was phased out.

Year	Population beginning of year	Total received	Transferred from other institutions	Other prisoners received (a)	Total discharged	Transferred to other institutions	Sentence expired	Conditionally released	Died (b)	By court order	Population end of year
1960.......	264	49	46	3	59	43	5	8	1	2	254
1959.......	288	62	54	8	86	66	2	15	2	1	264
1958.......	271	77	66	11	60	44	1	12	2	1	288
1957.......	277	42	31	11	48	30	2	9	2(c)	5	271
1956.......	297	74	60	14	94	70	5	18	1	-	277
1955.......	293	53	43	10	49	39	3	7	-	-	297
1954.......	255	95	75	20	57	39	4	10	-	4	293
1953.......	227	82	81	1	54	39	1	13	-	1	255
1952.......	230	33	33	-	36	23	1	11	1	-	227
1951.......	232	49	48	1	51	39	-	8	3	1	230
1950.......	222	59	58	1	49	40	1	7	1	-	232
1949.......	240	25	24	1	43	20	1	18	2	2	222
1948.......	248	30	30	-	38	17	3	17	1	-	240
1947.......	276	44	44	-	72	52	1	15	-	4	248
1946.......	274	40	39	1	38	23	1	6	6	2	276
1945.......	229	65	64	1	20	14	1	5	-	-	274
1944.......	248	29	29	-	48	27	4	13	2	2	229
1943.......	261	26	25	1	39	19	5	9	2	4	248
1942.......	282	40	40	-	61	47	3	8	2	1	261
1941.......	290	5	5	-	13	3	3	5	1	1	282
1940.......	288	71	71	-	69	58	1	8	-	2	290
1939.......	298	36	36	-	46	32	7	4	1	2	288
1938.......	302	51	50	1	55	36	6	6	5	2	298
1937.......	261	81	81	-	40	20	8	8	-	4	302
1936.......	242	65	65	-	46	33	5	-	3	5	261
1935.......	(d)	247	245	2	5	-	4	-	-	1	242

(a) 66 prisoners received from court, 1 violator of parole and 16 of conditional release, 1 prisoner who had escaped from another institution, 2 prisoners briefly at large on the island, and 1 other.

(b) Includes 1 in 1943 and 2 in 1938 presumed to have been killed by gunfire or drowned in attempting to escape. Also includes 1 drowned attempting escape, 1959.

(c) Includes 1 prisoner at large on island, captured within 24 hours.

(d) Alcatraz opened as a Bureau of Prisons institution in June, 1934.

52

Some of the prisoners lived to see the prison die, but after a century and more of service the lighthouse closing hurt more. The last keeper of the beacon that guided history through the Golden Gate relinquished his post to an automatic sentry.

U. S. PENITENTIARY
ALCATRAZ CALIFORNIA

NEXT HIGH NO. 1559		DATE: JUNE 13 1962	
MAXIMUM CAPACITY 336			
INMATES		EMPLOYEES	AUTH	ACTUAL

INMATES		EMPLOYEES	AUTH	ACTUAL
ANGLO	175	ADMINISTRATIVE	9	9
COLORED	75	ADVISORY	4	2
INDIAN	3	CULINARY	5	5
JAPANESE AND CHINESE	2	CUSTODIAL	99	94
MEXICAN	10	INDUSTRIES	12	12
PUERTO RICAN	1	MECHANICAL	28	29
		USPHS	5	5
TOTAL	266	TOTAL	162	156

O. G. BLACKWELL
WARDEN

Only once or twice was a prisoner stopped by a fence; the gates to the prison were not the elaborately cordoned portals designed by the penologists. As they were to learn in time, only the cold waters of the bay would be their walls. In the cold light of day it seems so obvious. But prisons have always had to have fences.

A prisoner's first look at his future home was during a walk, stark naked, down "broadway," the main corridor of the prison. Surely, this was the coldest welcome a man might experience. Few saw Cellblock A, identified by the spiral staircase; it was the oldest, reserved for a criminal population explosion that never came. When Scarface Al Capone made this trip, the Warden felt his job was half over.

AL CAPONE

MACHINE GUN KELLY

← LEFT- STAIRCASE
AT ALCATRAZ
RIGHT — MAIN
CELL BLOCK →

ALCATRAZ
PRISON

SAN
FRAN-
-CISCO
HARBOR

Machine Gun Kelly and Capone are perhaps the most famous graduates of the Rock, but lesser-knowns were far more difficult to handle. Kelly came to Alcatraz for kidnapping and was discovered to be one of the more docile of the inmates.

PRISONERS

Alcatraz, the prison, would never have come into being without a general breakdown in law enforcement by individual states in the late 1920's. "Gangsters and racketeers" were making a mockery of state police and state prisons. The Bonnie and Clydes of the day had money for bribes and expert legal advice. When they were convicted, they often escaped. And, when they couldn't escape, they were able to run their empires from behind bars. They were the darlings of newspaper headline writers. And, when they were assembled on the Rock from various federal penitentiaries around the country, they became news all over again. Behind all the glamor, however, their exploits seem small-time today. With the exception of a few who led charmed lives or who defied unbelievable confinement, their stories are depressing tales of losers.

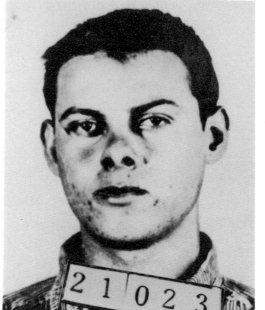

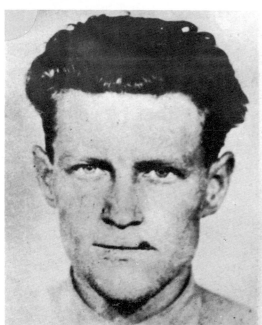

Their names were magic. Their faces merged into a composite:
"Doc," "Monk," "Dutch," "Chief," "Old Red," "Shorty," "Dusty." They were typically born in the nineteenth century and wound up in Alcatraz for robbing trains, the U.S. Mail and for killing when it meant freedom.

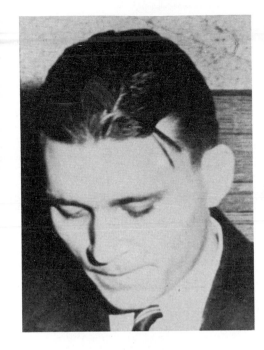   

  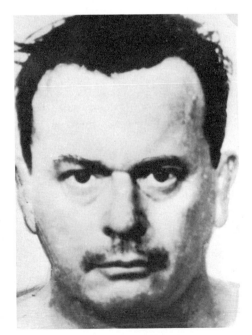 

Some would write the Warden later that Alcatraz had straightened them out. Others would say it drove men to insanity. Others, like Capone, would play the banjo, or like the "Birdman," study and play chess to make something human out of this half-life.

The lifeline to the island for supplies, doctors and visitors was the prison launch, which docked at the end of this San Francisco pier. Here prisoners left and re-entered the "free world." When the prison closed, the small building was taken over as a studio by author Barnaby Conrad. Today, it is all but unnoticed as another kind of cruise ship passes it by.

Robert Guilford

One of the few living tenants of The Rock comes back as a tourist and appropriately stands in the doorway of the library where he checked out and read some 15,000 books in his 12½-year stay in "the joint." But what Guilford remembers most vividly, he told us, is how he managed to survive "the hole."

"The hole" was a 9' x 5' steel box with no light or plumbing—a special form of solitary designed to punish the type of behavior Guilford fell into. In a rage of frustration, he turned on a lieutenant of the guards and beat him into insensibility in a matter of seconds. Guilford was thrown into "the hole" for 97 days, a week longer than the guard was in the hospital. Without clothes, with food consisting of two cups of water and a piece of bread daily and a "stew" twice a week, Guilford managed to put himself to sleep by walking in a circle until he collapsed on his knees and elbows.

In all, Guilford spent five years and three months in solitary. Between these stints, he learned to be a dental assistant and a baker. He prided himself on taking care of "The Birdman" Robert Stroud, whose entire prison term was spent in solitary as a condition of the commutation of his death sentence. Another of Guilford's famous friends was his next-door cellmate, Al Karpis, who, with the "Doc" Barker gang, participated in the kidnapping of the Hamms Brewery heir. It is said that when the San Francisco Giants' games were allowed to be broadcast on Alcatraz, Karpis was especially fond of the Hamms Jingle. Guilford spent 37½-years in various prisons paying his debt to society.

Clarence "Joe" Carnes and Robert Guilford came back to their hell to toast its demise, and to peer into Cellblock "A" which they had never seen. They could still joke about having outlived it. They could still visit the fog bell or the library like tourists.

Clarence "Joe" Carnes

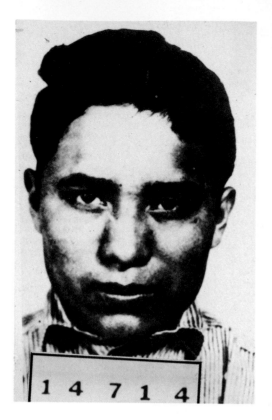

On May 2, 1946, Guard Earnest Lageson lay wounded in Cell 403 as the first day of the "Battle of Alcatraz" settled into night. As the searchlights played against the windows, he scribbled the names of the rebels on the wall. They were Cretzer, Coy, Hubbard, Shockley, Thompson, Carnes and Lageson who would live out the three-day siege among the bodies of two dying comrades. Cretzer, Coy and Hubbard would die, shell-shocked, frozen to their guns. Shockley and Thompson would go to San Quentin's gas chamber. Clarence Carnes, a Choctaw Indian from Oklahoma, was given a good word by one of the captive guards. He received only a life sentence to go along with his previous term of 99 years plus life for robbery, murder, kidnapping, assault and escape. He was 19 years old.

The "Choctaw Kid" had compressed all this into three years, beginning, as J. Campbell Bruce reports, with the delivery of a watermelon from his father to him in reform school. In the melon was a hacksaw.

Carnes is the only survivor of the Battle from the inside and perhaps one of the few to remember the drama that gripped the City those warm spring days several wars ago.

Roy Gardner

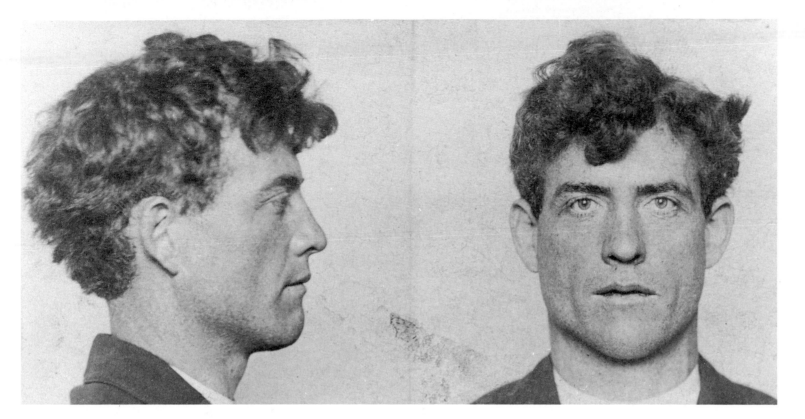

Men like Roy Gardner were born about a quarter of a century too soon for Alcatraz. Here was a criminal in the tradition of "Black Bart": a loner, he used guns only as a threat, robbed in broad daylight and was as elusive as a morning fog. In between mail robberies, his specialty, he did time in the Army, mined in Mexico and Kennett, California, sold World War I bonds to his fellow workers in a San Francisco shipyard and, after leaving Alcatraz, operated a "Crime Doesn't Pay" concession at the World's Fair on Treasure Island. Twice he escaped from two marshals accompanying him to the Federal Penitentiary at McNeil Island, Washington—in leg irons both times. In between these escapades, he brought notoriety to the Porter Hotel in Roseville, California by playing in an open poker game three days after bringing off two mail robberies just down the street. He then broke out of McNeil and traveled across the West leaving a trail of letters to a San Francisco newspaper with a garrulous account of his escape. From then on,

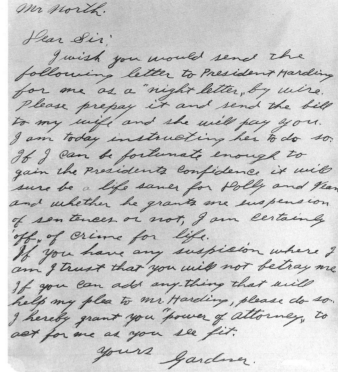

Gardner's story was one of frustration. From Leavenworth to Atlanta, he knocked his head against stone walls and was finally selected for the first guest list at the Rock. Now fifty years old, he began a new, industrious life. In less than four years he was out on parole and again captured headlines with a serialized life story. The part he would write a year later was in a suicide note, "I am old and tired and don't care to continue the struggle. Please let me down as light as possible."

The Roy Gardner saga is replete with touches of the Old West merging into a Jimmy Cagney prison melodrama. The San Francisco *Call Bulletin* reported the classic capture of Gardner in 1921. He was playing cards with "A. H. Smith, Fire Chief Al Ridley, and Slim Davis" in the East Side Bar in Roseville, 600 feet from the train station that was his entree to a series of mail robberies. He willingly led a posse to a cache in granite quarries (which had supplied stone for the Bank of Italy) 1500 feet off the highway, marked only by a broken tree, to recover the stolen mail sacks and keys.

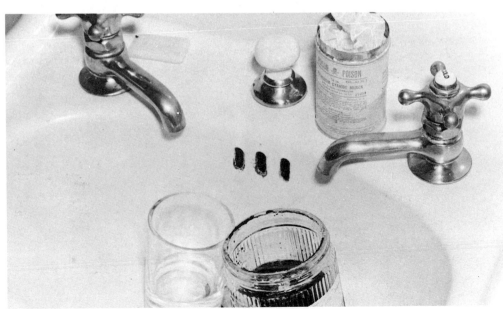
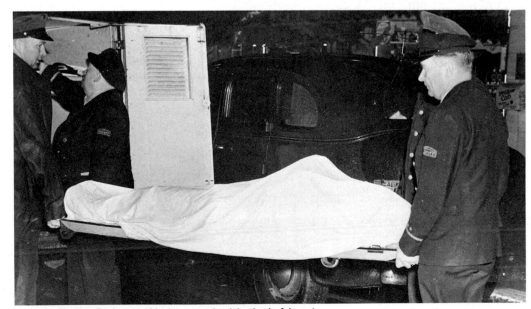

Gardner's letters, his relationship with his mother, with his wife Dolly, Dolores Wades, and with their friend Luis Sonney, his hopeful farewell from The Rock on parole in June of 1938 gave only a hint of the fate that he would choose: a whiff of cyanide fumes in his lonely room in the "free" world.

'46 Siege

Only the labyrinthine structure of the prison of Alcatraz could glamorize the futility of this elemental attempt at escape. The six participants had no chance. The guard towers were never threatened, the remaining convicts huddled in their cells until herded to the recreation yard and a flotilla of armed craft circled the island. No less than General Joseph, "Vinegar Joe," Stillwell and General Frank Merrill (Merrill's Marauders) stood behind Warden Johnston in his moment of trial. In the end, it was a Marine veteran of Guam who dropped demolition charges through holes in the roof of the main cellblock, which shattered any resistance.

The cumbersome inadequacies of the prison were revealed in this abortive breakout attempt. Prisoners could time the routine positions of guards. They could scale the cells to the gun gallery above. They could overpower a portion of the prison before an alert was sounded. Then, they could hold out doggedly and go down in heroic fireworks.

The excitement of a fight to the death intrigued San Franciscans for several days. Then the reality came home. There was no dark secret hidden in the revolt, despite the attempts of newspapers to fan the rumors of cruelty and neglect. If there was to be an escape, this was not the way to do it. If there was to be a protest, this was the type that would not be heard.

Attempted Break

The murder of a guard, Royal C. Cline, in a bloody breakout attempt in May, 1938, brought two convicts, Jimmy Lucas and Rufus Franklin, into a San Francisco courtroom for a headline-grabbing three-week trial. As Mrs. Etta Cline looked on, defense attorney Harold Faulkner tried to create a reasonable doubt that a hammer was the fatal bludgeon. The gruesome evidence—bullet fragments, a trail of blood, a death mask—led to conviction. The image of freedom-crazed convicts who would stop at nothing was now established.

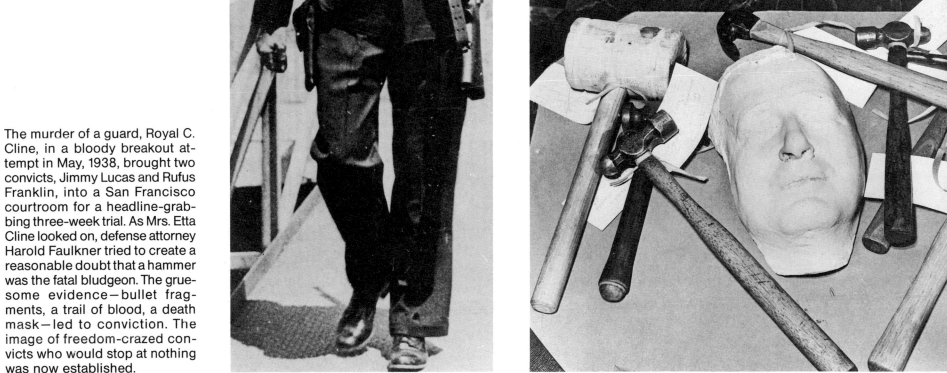

Escapes

The first test of The Rock's inner defenses came on December 16, 1937, when convicts Ted Cole and Ralph Roe disappeared from a work building and were never seen again—apparent victims of the Bay's icy waters. Kidnapper Arthur "Doc" Barker sawed out of his cell in January, 1939 but was stopped by a bullet on the water's edge. Warden Johnston prided himself in the "escape-proof" soubriquet of the prison and its specially trained guards, despite some mysterious disappearances unsolved to this day.

Last Escape

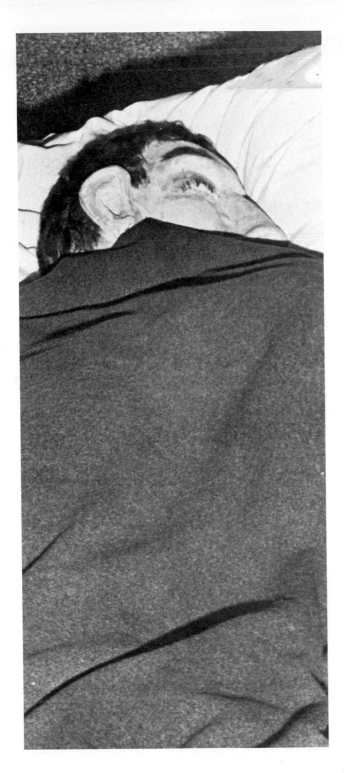

In 1962, with Warden Blackwell now in charge, Alcatraz was to receive its first and last professional escape attempt. It was obvious to Frank Morris and his fellow graduates from other Federal penitentiaries, John and Clarence Anglin, that a daytime break was the easiest way to get over walls but not off the island. Their plot began with a pick made from a spoon and a finger-nail clipper, welded together with book matches. For six months, they worked at an air vent, which opened to a utility corridor, then to the cellblock roof. In the course of their nocturnal labors, they fashioned a drill to chew off rivet heads, made *papier mâché* copies of the removed grill and fabricated masks complete with human hair. Armed with water wings, a raft, tide charts, cash and a list of addresses, they crept to the north shore of the island on June 11, 1962 and set out for Angel Island. The whole story of their escape plot was told in what they left behind, including clothes hanging over the empty vent in John Anglin's cell. The debris that was recovered contained everything except the three men. Attorney General Robert F. Kennedy flew to San Francisco to announce the phasing out of Alcatraz.

A final epitaph to the escape-proof myth of The Rock was written six months later, exactly 25 years to the day after the disappearance of Cole and Roe. John Paul Scott sawed his way out and swam in an improvised Mae West three miles to the San Francisco shore, at Fort Point. He was promptly captured.

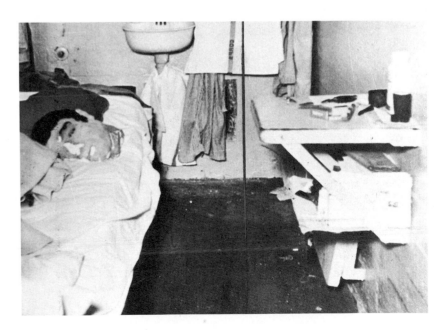

CLEAN YOUR PLATE
OR GO WITHOUT THIS
MEAL THE NEXT DAY

Alcatraz fired the imagination of 'thirties film makers, as "tough guys" paraded through roles of gangsters, framed innocents and women-hungry desperadoes. The Warner Brothers still at left is from "Alcatraz Island," remembered only for the girl who waited off shore, Ann Sheridan.

Neither realism nor social concerns animated these films. Yet leading studios and actors were attracted to this genre and continue to be. Most recently, "Escape From Alcatraz," retold the story of the 1962 attempt (page 71). Alcatraz has always been the most photogenic prison to have been built or imagined.

John Lytel, George E. Stone and Dick Purcell.

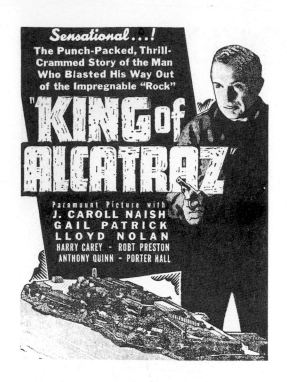

Joan Bennett in "House across the Bay."

The setting was Sing-Sing, but the feeling was Alcatraz, as George Raft squared off with Jimmy Cagney and with Lloyd Nolan, and Bogart posed in his chair. The fog-shrouded rock still drew the box office, the waiting, the mystery. Anthony Quinn got one of his first roles in "King of Alcatraz," but even with this cast, the film is forgotten today.

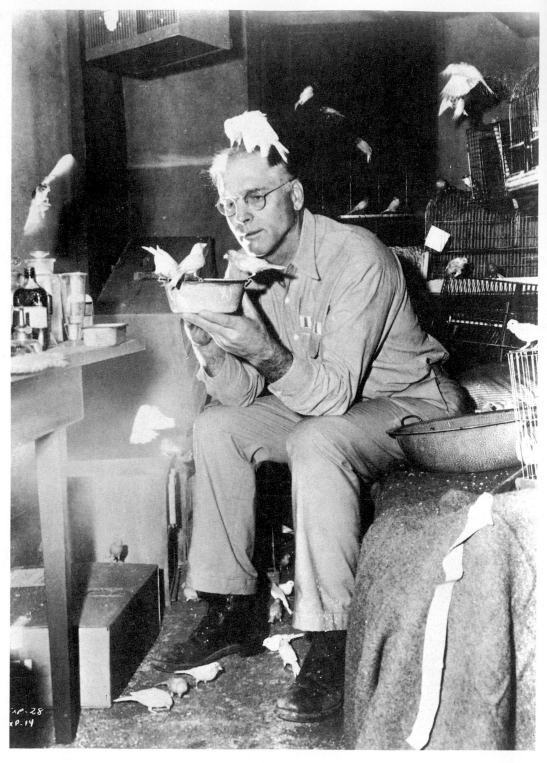

Robert F. Stroud—"The Birdman."

With *Birdman of Alcatraz* in 1962, an artistic breakthrough in prison films brought a human story to the screen. Burt Lancaster delivered one of his finest performances as Robert F. Stroud, who arrived at Alcatraz at the age of 52 after 33 years of prison terms. Stroud had been spared from hanging by Woodrow Wilson, became an expert in the diseases of birds and achieved a measure of professional fame. At the time of his death in 1963, he was a sympathetic figure and one of the heroes of The Rock.

Finally, as the convulsions of the closing of Alcatraz began to open up the prison, a major studio was allowed to move in to film, on location, "Point Blank." Lee Marvin starred. Before this, Alcatraz was forbidden territory for the press.

Alcatraz

(Photo: John Slavicek)

They made many promises, but kept only one.
They promised to take our land, and they took it.

OCCUPATION

There were other claims, but the American Indians, representing twenty tribes, seized Alcatraz on November 20th, 1969 with a well-thought-out vengeance after the prison was three years gone. The Indian claim does not stand up to historical fact—but then it was not a claim but a statement. While the debate went on about "what to do about Alcatraz," their decision was clear. They had an opportunity to stake a claim, and they did. Dennis Banks and his boarding parties met little opposition on the island. The guards were put ashore, and the Indians settled in, Gandhi-style, to a peaceful but very evident protest from 1969 until 1971. In 1972 Alcatraz island became part of the Golden Gate National Recreation Area.

The Bay Area responded to the cry of freedom of the Indians. At touristy Fisherman's Wharf, contributors lined up daily to fill the lifeline to Alcatraz. After some initial harassment, the claiming of the island settled down to a battle of wits and nerves. Would the government risk confrontation?

It was written on the walls; the Indians meant to stay. Venting their pent-up rage on the institution, they pillaged and burned the warden's home, the guards' apartments, the lighthouse keeper's home—here shown before (left) and after.

The bitterness continued. The "Feds" and the Indians sized each other up. Epithets were hurled, insults were scrawled on the cell block walls. Someone would have to give. Tension grew, but the federal government held back.

Sympathy for the Indian cause, in spite of the destruction of the island's landmarks, kept an armed confrontation away. Finally, facing a long siege and having made their point, the Indians withdrew.

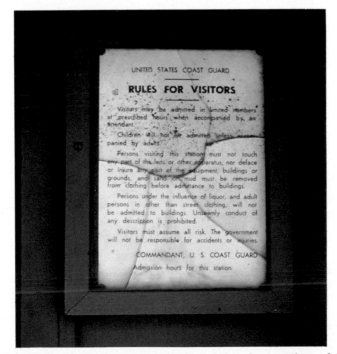

Sympathy for the Indian cause, in spite of the destruction of the island's landmarks, kept an armed confrontation away. Finally, facing a long siege and having made their point, the Indians withdrew.

PRESENT

The highrises of San Francisco now dwarf the orphan isle that once pretended to guard the city. More than a decade of allowing Alcatraz to fall into ruin has now passed. And while the entire Bay area searches for those last remaining acres to build on, it seems best to return the Rock to the birds who first gave it its name. Angel Island behind it, to the right, stands as a reminder that some parts of the Bay were never meant to be the habitat of man.

Another uniform, another spirit came over the island in 1972 when it was named as part of the Golden Gate National Recreation Area in the National Park System. The past was swept clear by the smiles of young guides. The future of Alcatraz was still up in the air, but at last someone had *seen* it. Another generation would have something to say. Still, there were people who felt that Alcatraz was an invitation to "do something."

Vacant Alcatraz on some days receives as many as 1,400 visitors. Flowers have begun blooming amid the ruins.

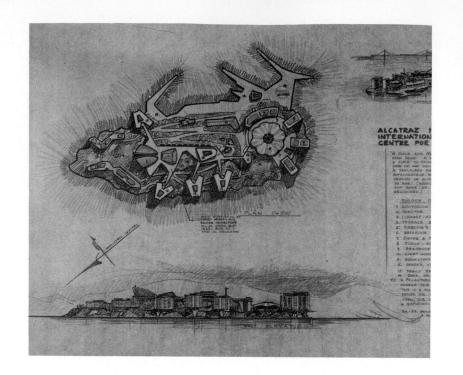

ALCATRAZ
INTERNATIONAL
CENTER FOR

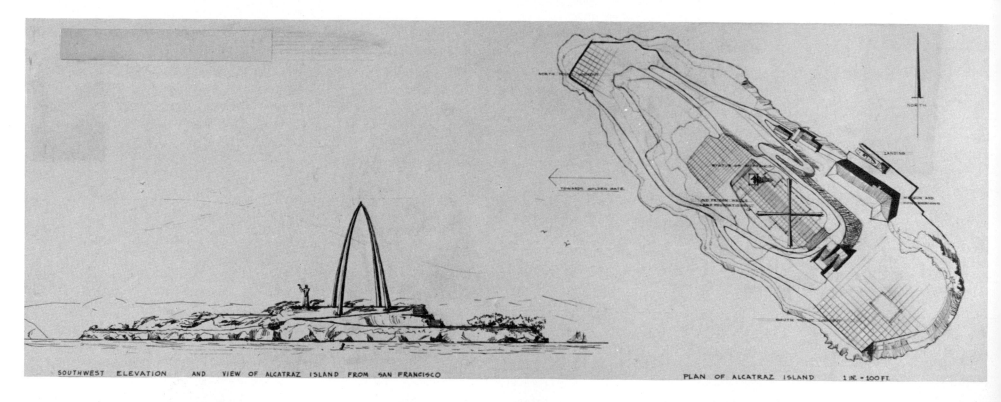

SOUTHWEST ELEVATION AND VIEW OF ALCATRAZ ISLAND FROM SAN FRANCISCO

PLAN OF ALCATRAZ ISLAND   1 IN. = 100 FT.

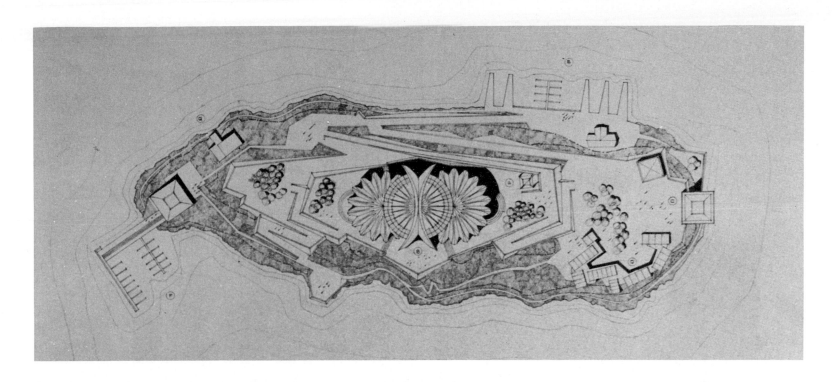

A contest for ideas for the future of Alcatraz produced every concept from a floating gambling hall to an Ellis Island of the Pacific. A Bufano monument might have been a comforting compromise, but, as Herb Caen has predicted, Alcatraz would remain only a memory and could not hope to be more.

The votive light of Alcatraz goes out. Dog, man, memory are replaced by another technology. The lighthouse is now remote-controlled. An oil slick can come as stealthily as an earthquake to envelope an environment, to prove even an island has to fight to survive.

All of this was Alcatraz. The tour boats are a footnote on history, a voyage into a bay that has intrigued explorers since the days of Sir Francis Drake.

Other books by Robert Cameron: ABOVE SAN FRANCISCO
ABOVE LOS ANGELES
ABOVE HAWAII
ABOVE WASHINGTON (D.C.)
ABOVE LONDON with Alistair Cooke
ABOVE YOSEMITE

These hardcover books are collections of Nostalgic and Contemporary Aerial Photographs in one hundred and sixty 11 x 14 inch full color pages for $19.95 available from the publisher or at fine booksellers.